How To Build
A
Garden Bench

TIMOTHY D. STEWART

Copyright © 2014 Timothy D. Stewart

ISBN-13: 978-1499168419
ISBN-10: 1499168411

Timothy D. Stewart
Visit my website at www.mrstilts.com

INTRODUCTION

If you are a novice woodworker then this project is a great way to practice your woodworking or hone up your skills. If you have never built anything, then by all means give this project a try. You are hereby warned; you may become an avid woodworker. There is nothing better than knowing you built it yourself.

This is one project that will not break the bank and give you years of enjoyment. It's heavy enough to withstand a good wind too!

The 2x4 Garden Bench uses the most basic carpentry skills. It's fast to construct and easy to maintain. For those more seasoned woodworkers or DIY enthusiasts you may find yourself making multiple ones for friends and family. My daughters have their order in already!

Now for the cost, the best part! I constructed this one for under $40.00 (excludes your finishing choice – as of 2013) using construction grade 2x4's. If you have access to economy grade 2x4's you could even build this 2x4 Garden Bench for less. When selecting your lumber, make sure you choose boards with minimal knots or at least small knots. The other area of concern is whether the boards are warped or twisted. If any of them are twisted put them back on the pile.

Now I built my Garden Bench utilizing construction grade 2x4's. You may even want to consider purchasing treated lumber. That's great it will last even longer. If you do decide to go this avenue just remember the overall cost of the project will increase and you may have to wait until the lumber dries to apply your finish. Treated lumber tends to be wet so cutting the lumber may take a little longer if you are using hand tools. The main advantage; this type of lumber will outlast most construction grade 2x4's.

Should you select any boards or any of your purchased boards become slightly warped, this is usually not a problem. Since you will be gluing and nailing them to another board, the warp or bow is usually removed.

This is the best part of the Garden Bench design, especially if you are only using a hand saw!

NO PRIOR WOODWORKING SKILLS REQUIRED!

CONTENTS

UPCOMING PROJECTS

Upright Planter

I first saw a similar planter in one of my garden magazines so I hopped online and did some research. I found an array of styles that DIY'ers said worked.

Since I have limited sun for growing strawberries I decided to try my hand at building one. Well I can say "YES" it does work. The vines you are seeing are first year strawberry plants.

The planter is portable with heavy duty casters and has PVC piping throughout that delivers the water evenly.

Virtually no maintenance, I have yet to weed it!

Shadow Box

This shadow box frame was constructed of construction grade 2x6's and 3/8" thick popular shelves.

This unit is hung by using (4) 16lb command strips. As you can see I had no problem trusting this method. The shadow box has been mounted for several years now. The key is to purchase the right hanger. This type of hanging systems is not for everyone nor am I saying it works on all wall surfaces. Choose a hanger that fits your style and project

.

Floating Shelf

Now here is one fun project that will generate questions from your guest. Don't be surprised if you are asked time and time again "where did you buy that".

No power tools ... No problem ...

Child's Rocking Chair

Have even updated these plans since I drew them up. Now printing space theme designs on the frame. My plans and patterns are being updated.

Recessed Shelf

This weekender project is both elegant and functional. Depending upon your choice of lumber and finish the unit can conform to most decor's.

This one is built using popular for the frame and a oak plywood back. Popular takes stain easy and is easy to sand.

It's designed to fit between your wall studs. The shelving units are adjustable making it very versatile.

Concrete Table Lamp

Concrete, it's not for sidewalks anymore! When I first proposed making a lamp out of concrete my wife looked at me like I was CRAZY!

Famous quote; "I do not want a hunk of concrete on my end table".

The specks you are seeing in the charcoal colored concrete are bits of stained glass. The top and bottom wood pieces are reclaimed lumber out of old barns.

I'll take you step by step through the entire process.

Just for the record this lamp is now on a certain individuals end table!

More upcoming concrete projects;

- Concrete Planter
- Concrete End Table
- Concrete Outdoor Bench

All completed projects have high quality images at www.mrstilts.com.

1 GARDEN BENCH PHOTO'S

Now as you can see from the image of the finished Garden Bench I have installed spacers under the feet. This was really for photo purposes, however I decided to take it one step further.

I purchased the same spray being advertised to seal rain gutters. I flipped the bench over and with painters tape, taped off about 3" of leg back from the end. Then completely coated the end of the leg assembly.

2 DESIGN CONCEPT

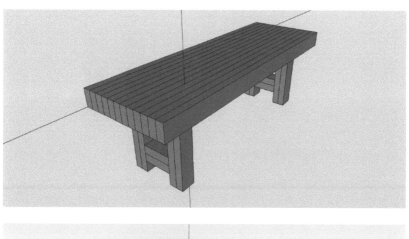

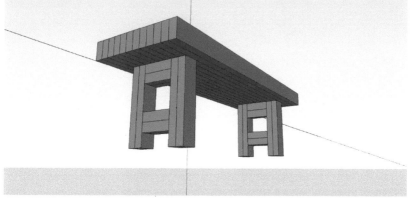

Style A

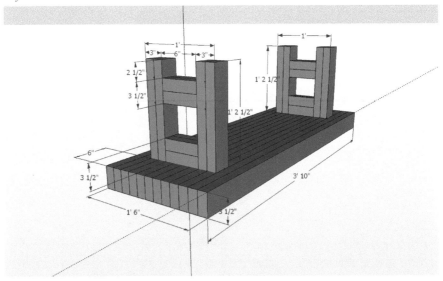

Material List (Style A)

8 - 2"x4"x8' studs (common or treated)
1 - 16 oz. bottle of TiteBond Glue III or equivalent
1.5lb - Exterior grade #16 nails
1.5 lb - Exterior grade screws (optional)
1 Variety pack of sand paper (60-80-100-120 grit)

Material Cut List

Bench Top
12 - 2"x4"x46" studs

Bench Legs
8-2"x4"x14 1/2"
8-2"x4"x6"

Style A - Optional Leg Assembly Brace

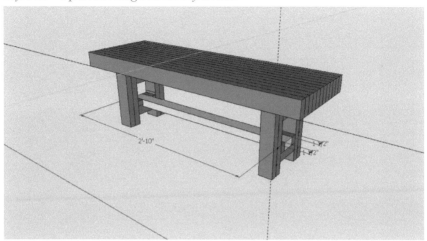

Material List (Style A)

9 - 2"x4"x8' studs (common or treated)
1 - 16 oz. bottle of TiteBond Glue III or equivalent
1.5lb - Exterior grade #16 nails or screws (optional)
1 - Variety pack of sand paper (80-100-120 grit)

Materiel Cut List

<u>Bench Top</u>
12 - 2"x4"x46" studs

Style B

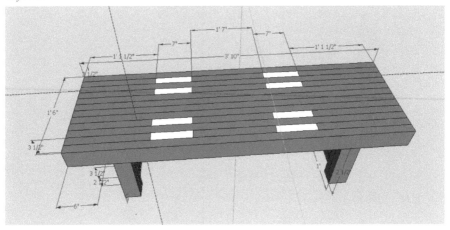

Material List (Style B)

8 - 2"x4"x8' studs (common or treated)
1 - 16 oz. bottle of TiteBond Glue III or equivalent
1.5lb - Exterior grade #16 nails
2 bxs - Exterior grade screws (optional)
1 - Variety pack of sand paper (80-100-120 grit)

Material Cut List

Bench Top
12 - 2"x4"x46" studs
8 - 2"x4"x1'-11/2"
4 - 2"x4"x1'-7"

Bench Legs
8-2"x4"x14 1/2"
6-2"x4"x6"

NOTE: If you are going to use the cross brace between the legs you need to alter the cut list.

Style B - Layout Diagram

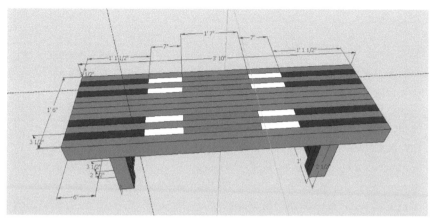

The light and dark gray merely represent the different spacers for Style B. The white colored sections represent the opening between the studs.

The only advantage to this style is it allows water to drain through the bench. Just make sure you apply some paint to the 2x4's where the openings are or it will rot quickly.

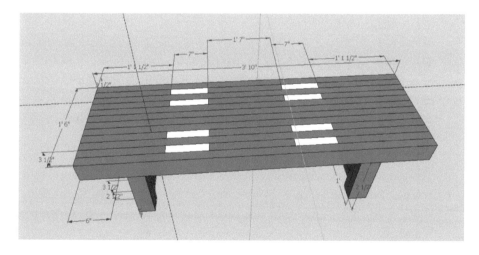

Take your time and measure carefully when building this Garden Bench. When assembling this style you will have a few more pieces than if you assembled a solid bench.

3 GENERAL INFORMATION

Framing Square

This is one of the most basic tools that will assist you over and over. It's easy to use and some are adjustable. You will most likely require a couple of sizes, for me I actually own a 6", 13", and 24".

Selecting Lumber

For those readers who have never purchased lumber it can be difficult sometimes to get perfectly straight boards. Let's take a 2"x4"x8" stud, to determine if the board is usable lay it flat (wide side) down. Take a step back and see if it rises off the floor or lays flat and whether the board looks like a snake.

Now repeat the process with the board laying up on edge. This is a great way to determine if the board is usable. Try always selecting the best boards; if you do have a couple slightly warped or become warped after you get them home, do not fret; you should be able to use them somewhere in your project.

Miter box

There are a number of companies that produce basic to high end miter boxes. Since I had an upper end one I used that, actually it was my dad's at one time. As for the basic, nothing wrong with them, for more complex cuts or precision cutting the basic one may or may not fit the bill.

Safety Precautions

This goes without saying, always follow the safety guidelines for every tool you use. From hand tools to power tools you need to operate them safely and properly. Eye and hearing protection is always recommended anytime it is needed.

Failure to follow safety precautions could lead to an unwanted accident! We assume no liability for the misuse of tools.

Excess Glue Clean Up

Wipe off any excess glue, to clean an area simply dampen a paper towel or rag and wipe off the excess glue careful not to wipe off all the glue you just put in the seam.

Whatever you are using, your towel should not be dripping with water; too much water will raise the grain in the wood. So squeeze out excess water.

Also if you have wiped excess glue off and happen to have smeared it a damp rag or towel can be utilized to clean the residue off.

After you're satisfied with the entire Garden Bench you could lightly sand the top, although it may not be necessary, this will eliminate any raised grain should you have used too much water.

4 TOOL LISTING

Hand Tools

- Hammer (straight or curved claw)
- Handsaw
- Miter Box (optional) - You can purchase your saw with the miter box.
- Framing Square - 12" or 24"
- Electric Drill (optional but makes life easier)

Power Tools - Optional

- Air Compressor
- Air Nail Gun
- Chop Saw
- Circle Saw
- Reciprocating Saw
- Electric Drill

5 CONSTRUCTION PROCESS

(Style A) Construction

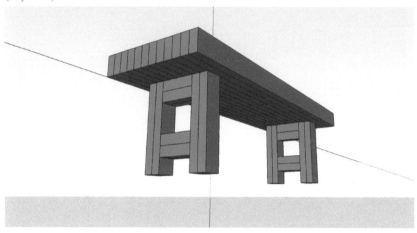

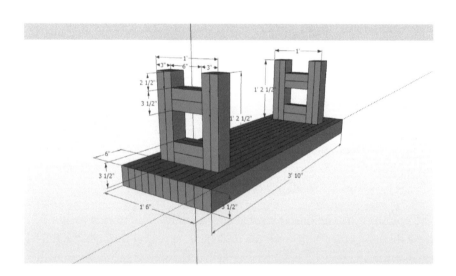

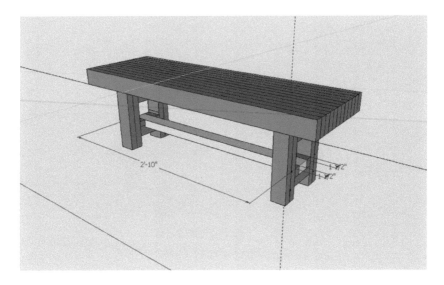

If you decide that you would like the extra bracing (represented by the white colored 2x4) then you will need to cut a few extra pieces.

Notice the small pieces on either side of the 2x4. These are 1 1/2" wide and are placed on each side of the brace. Now securing them will be a little tricky.

Small pieces of lumber like this are easy to split and hard to nail given their location. My recommendation would be to make this complete cross brace and support first before securing it to the legs. If you don't it will be difficult to secure the small pieces to the lower leg support.

One option is to assemble as normal and when it's time to either nail or screw them together do it from the underside, screwing through the full leg brace or use a couple of small adjustable bar clamp and secure them with glue.

For even more support repeat the above process and install a cross member directly under the bench top.

Material and Cut List

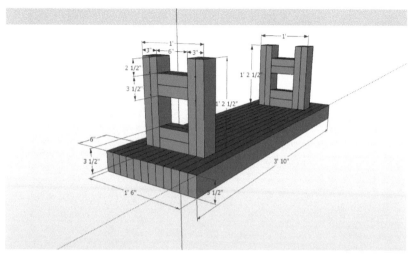

Material List (Style A)

8 - 2"x4"x8' studs (common or treated)
1 - 16 oz. bottle of TiteBond Glue III or equivalent
1.5lb - Exterior grade #16 nails
1.5 lb - Exterior grade screws (optional)
1 Variety pack of sand paper (60-80-100-120 grit)

Material Cut List

Bench Top
12 - 2"x4"x46" studs

Bench Legs
8-2"x4"x14 1/2"
8-2"x4"x6"

6 CUTTING THE LUMBER

Cutting The Lumber (Style A)

Bench Top

Let's begin by cutting the (12) 46" inch long pieces that when assembled will become the top or the seating area of the Garden Bench.

Now I utilized a chop saw, for those of you that only have a hand saw or circle saw the process may take a little longer, however the principles are all the same.

With a tape measure hook the end of the tape measure over the end of the 2"x4"x8' and mark a line at 46". If you are new to this you may want to use a framing square and draw your line across the 2"x4".

This also will aide you in maintaining a straight cut if you are using a circle saw or even a hand saw. If you are using a hand saw my recommendation would be to purchase a miter box (you can purchase miter boxes with a saw).

Now with the chop saw OFF (always follow safe work practices) I brought the blade down and aligned it just left of the mark. I never cut on the line, I always leave a shade visible.

As you can see the blade is just nudging the mark across the 2"x4".

I generally leave a little bit of the pencil mark when I cut. Then I raised the blade up, squeezed the trigger and eased my way through the 2"x4". I let the saw do the cutting; you do not need to force the blade through. If you do, you could end up splintering the wood, pinching the blade, or even worse getting injured.

If you are uneasy around power tools either cut all the lumber by hand or have an experienced carpenter cut the lumber for you. This is not a guide on how to use power tools I am merely providing guidance on the construction of the Garden Bench.

I repeated this process until (12) 46" long pieces were cut. These will be used to make the solid portion of the bench top. I stacked the newly cut boards off to the side and moved on to the next pieces on the list.

Always follow the safety precautions for any tool you are using.

Bench Legs

Now it's time to cut the boards that will become the legs, this will consist of (8) pieces cut at 14 1/2" in length. I measured from the right to left so I will be cutting along the left side of the line. Notice the full line rather than a mark; I used a framing square to draw a line all the way across.

Since I was cutting to the left of the line it was beneficial to me to have a full line this time, that's where a small framing square comes in handy. Notice the blade is just touching the line. Like above I always leave a little bit of pencil mark when I perform the cut.

With your first leg cut at 14 ½" you can use this piece to mark the remainder of the boards; makes your job a little faster. Align it up with the end of your 2"x4" and draw a line across with a marker, pen, pencil, etc. as indicated in the photograph. This should ensure your legs are all the same size.

You will need to repeat this step until you have cut (8) 14 1/2" pieces. Then it will be time to move onto the horizontal braces that will not only hold the legs straight but bring the whole project together.

When you have cut all the 14 ½" pieces; set them aside.

By not forcing the blade you can see how clean a cut is produced. Also as a reminder to anyone using a chop saw keep vigilant to where your fingers are, don't wear loose clothing, and always where your safety glasses.

When you complete a cut, let the saw blade stop before removing the newly cut piece. It is recommended that after releasing the trigger you let the blade completely stop.

Support Braces

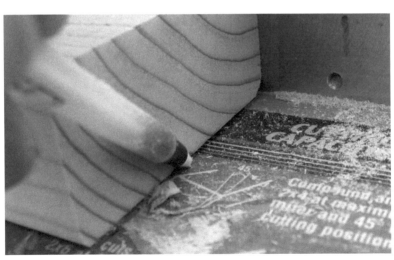

Let's move on to cutting the leg support braces.

Once again measure from the end of the board and mark your line at 6". You will be cutting the boards in the same fashion as you have for all the previous boards.

Now if you're using a chop saw you can mark your base with a pencil or blue painters tape to make the process quicker.

With the saw OFF I brought the blade down and took a tape measure and butt it up to the blade. I measured over 6" to the right and marked a line on the base (similar to the previous photo).

Now, after I move the board into the cutting position, I will be butting the end of the 2"x4" to the mark; then I will make the cut. This saves a little time when cutting multiple pieces such as these 6" pieces.

I repeated the process (8) times until I had all the leg support braces needed to complete the Garden Bench.

With all your lumber cut to the design dimensions or if you have modified the design to your dimensions you should have a pile such as indicated in the photo.

Yup just a stack of 2x4's!

7 GARDEN BENCH ASSEMBLY

Now that you have all the lumber cut to make your first Garden Bench separate your boards to be used as the top. For me this is the best part of the project, you finally get a feel for what your project will look like.

Garden Bench Top - Layout

Now let's begin the assembly process, first lay all the 46" long pieces on a flat surface. Here you will be checking the condition of the sides of the cut

2x4's. You want the smoothest side for the top and the sides of the bench.

If any of the boards are slightly bowed upward you push downward on them while you are nailing them in place. Forcing them flat to the surface and secured tightly with nails or screws.

Now that you have all the boards lined up it is time to begin the gluing and nailing. Do not nail to close to the edge of the board unless you drill a pilot hole, it will or most likely will, split.

Take each outside board and turn them outward like the photo (recommendation only).

Now mark an arrow to indicate the direction of the top side of the board; such as the one in the photo.

I did this just to keep a reference point and to remind me which side of the board is the top. When you begin gluing it is easy to forget which side is the better side.

Now don't be surprised if you generate a little bit of public interest at this point. I was surprised just how many motorist and walkers watch what I am building. In fact I had several motorist stop by just to see if I was going to be selling any of the benches.

I declined the offer, I make my projects for family only.

Bench Top - Glue Application

With all the boards aligned you want to make sure that when you are assembling them they remain fairly square. Notice I said fairly, things happen and boards can shift. I would recommend anyone to use a framing square throughout the assembly process.

You can also mark a line across your table top or board that is supporting your work to use as a reference point.

Another option is to screw down or clamp a 2"x4" straight across your work surface and then butt your 46" pieces tight to it during assembly. Add a second 2"x4" at a 90 degree angle to the first using a framing square and securely fasten it to the work surface. This way you will be able to maintain a square table with little problems. If you don't want to screw them down then utilize a couple of clamps to securely hold the 2"x4"'s in place.

This really is the easiest to do although can't say I did that.

Now stack the boards up and out of the way, are you glad you marked them now? Take the first outward board and add a bead of glue.

If you're unsure how much glue to add; error on more not less you can wipe the excess off.

You will continue this process until all the boards have been securely fastened to each other. Just keep repeating the process and finally you will have a secure and hefty Garden Bench Top.

As you are gluing the boards they will want to shift or slide, that's why it is best to have a brace secured to your work top to assist you in keeping them square.

Bench Top - Nailing

Remember you are also nailing these boards together using 16d or heavier nails, the glue is additional strength. Keep repeating the process until you have all the boards nailed and glued together.

There is no set spacing requirement for nailing, my rule of thumb is to space them approximately 6" apart.

If this is your first project then make it easy on yourself. Take your board and start your nails (screws if you prefer) then lay the board down against your square table top support and begin nailing. Once you have several nails partially into the adjoining board you can flip them up like I did in the photo.

Well you have just finished your first Garden Bench top or seating area. At this point, it is time to move onto the support legs and braces.

Notice the ends of the boards in the photo there are a few gaps created either from not nailing tight to the end (if you do remember it is very easy to split) or from some boards warping. If you want you can fill these areas with an exterior grade filler or glue (I usually use glue).

If you are painting this Garden Bench then either way yields great results. If you are staining the bench the glue may hinder stain application depending upon your brand.

Bench Legs - Layout

When you assemble the legs you can use your finished bench top as a straight edge. Once again always dry fit your boards just to make sure everything is lining up properly. Now go ahead and add the glue to the end of the 6" board wedged between the two 14 ½" boards.

Do not glue or nail the second 6" board in place at this time. The board in the (smaller pic) photo is only there to keep the right space between the leg braces so you can assemble them.

Here is where it may get tricky, since at this point you have no choice but to nail close to the edge, the board may split. If you are using an air nail gun the risk is reduced.

For those of you that are hand nailing you may want to drill a pilot hole through the outer board and partially into the 6" brace before nailing them in place (highly recommended).

If the board splits to much you may be better off ditching it and cutting a new one. Slight splits can sometimes be remedied by adding extra glue when you nail the outer leg brace in place.

As a visual reference for the assembly of the leg support, measure in 6" from the end of the Garden Bench and mark a line (the legs are recessed in 6" from each side of the bench). With a framing square draw a line all the way across.

This will be the guide line for the outer portion of the leg. Notice in the photo above there are exactly three 2"x4"x46" boards on each side of the leg support assembly.

Bench Legs - Gluing & Assembly

Move the leg assembly out of the way and add some glue between the joints as indicated. You will be lining up the legs along the line you made earlier with your framing square.

This will ensure a great fit when you securely fasten the leg assembly in place.

Then add the glue to the bottom of the top.

Now that you have the placement correct for your leg support assembly, it is time to glue and nail (or screw) in place. If you are using screws (drill a pilot hole) make sure you are using exterior grade and for support at least 3" (preferably 3 1/2").

With your leg assembly upside down add your glue. Do not go lightly on the glue.

Place the assembly back into position and hold in place for a couple of minutes (time varies depending upon air temperature), the glue will start to set and make it easier to add the nails or screws (when using screws its best to pre-drill).

If the glue is not set the assembly may slide a little, just work with it you will be able to hold it in place. I secured mine with three nails, try to make sure your nails are hitting the boards and not in a joint. I was close to the joint with the middle nail, hey no body is perfect.

Now that your assembly is secured you may be wondering if you did anything wrong or that the design is off. I assure you it's not, the assembly at this point is weak. When you add the remainder of the 6" braces and allow the glue to cure it will strengthen.

Garden Bench Legs - Gluing and Nailing

Let's start to complete the leg assembly by adding the remainder of the 6" boards. As indicated above add some glue to the assembly and place another 6" board directly on top then nail in place.

I nailed both down from the top and along the ends in the same fashion when I built the assembly.

Now drill a pilot hole (optional), however it does make it a lot easier if you do. It also decreases the chances that the board will split. If this board does split I would highly recommend replacing it with a new one.

Take four of the 6" cross pieces add glue to one side of two of them, similar to the photo.

Now place two of these pieces together, nail or screw in place. If any glue seeps out just wipe it off.

You will end up with two double braces that will complete your leg assembly. You're getting closer to the best part, finishing your Garden Bench.

If you are considering adding a leg cross brace then these blocks will vary slightly. See Style A - Optional Leg Assembly Brace section.

Now let's mark the 2"x4"x14 ½" leg assembly down 2" from the end or the bottom of the leg. This will be the location of the first 6" cross piece, do this on both inside legs.

To further ensure you are square, take a framing square and draw a line all the way across the board.

Smear some glue on the ends of the assembled 6" blocks and insert them between the two 14 ½" legs. You may need to spread the two sides slightly, take it easy here remember the glue has not dried yet. Once the block is located along the mark you placed 2" down from the end take your nails or screws and secure it in place.

Add some glue and fill any gaps that may be present between the leg and any of the blocks both upper and lower.

This will add strength and you really only have one shot to do this. Although when finished you can add glue in gaps the best adhesion is wood to wood.

At this time you will now spread glue on the remainder of the 14 ½" pieces and secure them to the legs previously installed. Make sure you add glue to only the one end that will rest against the bottom of the Garden Bench. Although not visible in this photo, add glue where the end of the support meets the bottom of the garden bench top.

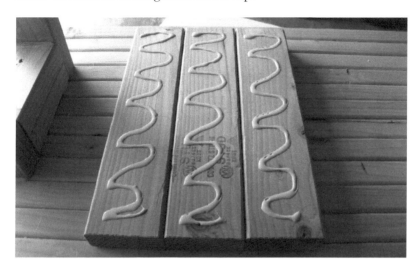

At this time you will now spread glue on the remainder of the 14 ½" pieces and secure them to the legs previously installed. Make sure you add glue to only the one end that will rest against the bottom of the Outdoor Bench.

Although not visible in this photo, add glue where the end of the support meets the bottom of the garden bench top.

With the glue on the boards you are simply going to place them against the outside legs and nail into place. Make sure you have placed some glue where the end of the board comes into direct contact with the bottom of the Garden Bench. Then either nail or screw them into place. When all the parts are dry (as per glue manufacturers recommendations), about 48 hours the legs will be very strong.

If you are in doubt and want added support, such as a cross brace; you can add the brace at this time. If you want more clean look just refer to Style A - Optional Leg Assembly Brace section.

8 SURFACE PREPARATION

Garden Bench Surface Preparation

Now that you have all the pieces assembled you should go around the legs and fill any gaps with a bead of glue.

Remember this is the bottom of the Garden Bench so if the glue smears I wouldn't worry about it (depending on finish).

Garden Bench Sanding

This step is optional, but for me I wanted rounded corners at the end of the Garden Bench. Sharp corners not only scrape but can splinter easier than rounded ones.

To do this I used an oscillating sander, however you could just as easy hand sand or use a sanding block. The photo is what it looks like when sanded over completely.

As you can see from the photo I used an orbital sander to finish the edges of the Garden Bench. I wanted to make sure that these edges were smooth to the touch. Smooth edges should not catch any clothing or be sharp or jagged when finish coated. I angled the sander about 45 degrees to get the desired angle. In addition I sanded the ends of the Outdoor Bench in the same fashion.

The finish does not have to be perfect, however smoothing the ends aides in the cosmetics and comfort of the bench, especially when you want to move it around.

You could easily do this by using sand paper or a sanding sponge. Remember if you are painting the Garden Bench you can get away with a rougher grit than staining. I used 80 grit sandpaper to sand to smooth the edges and ends.

9 FILLING THE VOIDS

Optional

It is almost impossible not to have some gaps between the ends and the finished top of the Garden Bench. I had some gaps that were wider than I would like, I filled these with Titebond III weather resistant glue.

Make sure that if any of the gaps go completely through the Garden Bench you run some painters tape up the seam along the bottom of the Garden Bench. This way your glue will stay in between and not drip out.

- You can also mix the glue with some saw dust created from your sanding. Mix it to a putty consistency and then using a putty knife force it between the gaps.

You may have to run some up the end seams also if your gaps are close to the end. Glue will shrink and ooze in further, so you may have to repeat this step several times.

Wipe off any excess glue, to clean an area simply dampen a paper towel and wipe up the access careful not to wipe off all the glue you just put in the seam. The paper towel should not be dripping with water; too much water will raise the grain of the wood. After you're satisfied with the entire Garden Bench you could lightly sand the top, although not necessary, this will eliminate any raised grain should you have used too much water.

A reminder before finishing the bench, make sure it has had ample time for the glue to dry. Always follow the manufacturer's recommendations.

I allowed 48 hours for curing based upon the type of glue and the air/humidity level. If the glue is soft or pliable then by all means let the Garden Bench dry another day. You do not want to apply paint or stain until the glue has cured.

10 PAINTING THE GARDEN BENCH

Garden Bench Finishing

Now you can either paint or stain your Garden Bench. Each has its own pro's and con's. For me I chose to paint my Garden Bench.

It allows me the opportunity to change the color of the bench, should I choose to do so. Just keep in consideration that high quality finishes last longer.

Painting

I chose to finish my Garden Bench with a latex based primer and paint. I am using a separate primer since the overall cost is less expensive than buying it as a primer/paint combination. I always opt for high quality products at slightly higher retail cost.

I will be using a brush rather than a roller. The brush will allow me to work my paint into the grooves of the lumber. You can always utilize a roller over the finished paint after your satisfied that any voids have been properly painted. The roller does produce a smoother finish.

Staining

Now you could stain the Garden Bench with great results. The multiple types of stains I have used in the past, transparent and semitransparent. All yield great results! Another option would be to utilize a solid stain, for this bench most likely the best choice.

If you select semi or transparent you may want to sand the bench further. If not, any imperfections will show through the stain. Both of these stains can show the imperfections of the bench whereas the solid colored stain usually hides them all.

Painting The Finished Garden Bench

Now for the painting, make sure you have selected paint that was manufactured for outdoor use. Sounds simple but one can forget, at least until you get home and have to go back to the store. Also purchase high quality paint, you will not regret it.

Unless you are using the primer when you first get home, you probably will have to stir the primer before use. If you are going to use the paint immediately make sure wherever you purchased the paint has thoroughly mixed it. It saves time and does a better job, no offense.

Since I purchased my primer one day and built the Garden Bench the next I had to remix my primer (although it was originally mixed by the home center).

When you first open the can after it has set (for long periods) you may notice liquid has accumulated along the surface of the paint. Very slowly stir using a clean mixing stick (usually free where you purchased your primer or paint) and in circular motions start mixing the liquid. Make sure to scrape along the bottom of the can. When it is mixed, it will appear similar to the photo, smooth in consistency.

I preferred to use a 4" brush, that's totally up to you. Since this is a large project it took me less time to cover the entire Garden Bench.

Do yourself a favor and do not overload the brush, it's easy to do. You will end up with more of a mess and if it is warm outside the excess paint could clump.

As you can see from photo's I dipped the brush in about 1 ½" and then lightly wiped one edge a bit.

This is where there are a lot of opinions, just how much paint should remain on the brush. Well, it's all up to you! I prefer to minimize dripping from the brush so I do lightly wipe off one side of the brush.

You can start anywhere I preferred to start on the underside of the Garden Bench (recommended for novice painters).

Make sure to work the paint into any cracks and crevices. More than likely you will have to do this twice, sometimes three times.

When you are applying paint, work it in with the brush and then lightly draw your brush down the surface in one direction.

If you do not, often you will have unsightly brush strokes showing up in the finish. Thus, the reason for starting on the underside, for those newbie's to woodworking or painting.

Notice the area where the legs meet the base, in one photo there where areas that did not receive any paint.

With this coat most all areas are now covered with primer. Keep working it until you have covered all areas of the bench.

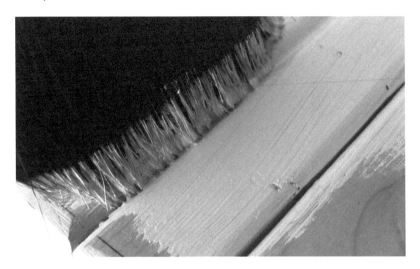

In some instances it is necessary to apply paint across the grain. This Garden Bench is difficult to cover all the surfaces without doing this.

Just remember to always remove your cross grain brush stroke by apply your brush lightly and draw your brush in one direction only.

After completing the end I painted the legs in the same fashion. The legs will take a little time; work the paint in the same direction of the lumber. Make sure to fill the gaps as much as possible with paint.

Here the end has been completely covered and I have started to work down the sides. If for any reason you need to switch sides or your paint is drying quickly, just make sure you keep your brush strokes going in the desired direction.

I have completed the first coat of primer, since it was very hot that day I planned on applying the second coat 2 hours later. Now you can clean your brush per manufacturer's directions or you can temporarily cover the brush.

This is not for everyone, but for me a zip lock bag works great. Oh, I almost forgot store the brush in a dark area. Remember this is a temporary measure, if you leave it to long the paint will dry.

11 GARDEN BENCH COMPLETED

Garden Bench - Primed & Ready for Paint

Here the Garden Bench has been completely covered with two coats of primer. This is also where I stop my instructional verbiage; the process for applying the finish coat (2 coats) is not any different than applying the primer.

Hope you found this guide helpful, I will have more designs and affordable projects coming soon.

This concludes this guide, I didn't think you needed to see me apply the finished coat of paint. Hope you have or had fun constructing your first Garden Bench.

Check out the upcoming projects under the introduction section (Upcoming Projects).

Just completed my first child's rocking chair!

ABOUT THE AUTHOR

Well there are a number of individuals, not to be named, that would call me the project master. Not sure if that is good or bad, but for the recipients of my projects, well, I have never had one turned down.

Throughout our home there are numerous handmade pieces of furniture ranging from country to fine art. There isn't much I won't tackle when it comes to creating the unusual. There is nothing more rewarding than creating with your own two hands. Anyone can purchase something, but for some of us we prefer to build it ourselves.

My goal with my Weekender Project series is simple, provide an easy to build project that can be built in a weekend. Sounds simple enough, well at least that's what I thought! As a seasoned woodworker I had to take a step back. Not everyone has even lifted a hammer before, so my designs are based upon that concept.

For those experienced woodworkers you may find my guide to simple. Great ...

There is no guarantee in life but I do feel that you will have a fighting chance of experiencing the joy of woodworking. With power tools you will find yourself completing the Garden Bench assembly in a morning. Anyone using hand tools will find that they will need a little longer but this can be built in a weekend!

Make sure you visit the Upcoming Projects section! I have a number of projects planned for you. Projects that will range in difficulty, to challenge the more experienced DIY'er. I believe the most simplest project of them all is my Floating Shelves. Not only are they simple you can make them as elegant as you would like.

The most difficult and time consuming project will be the Polished Concrete Lamp! That's right concrete, it's not just for sidewalks anymore!

Stay tuned for more projects to come, you can visit my website at www.mrstilts.com.

Lightning Source UK Ltd.
Milton Keynes UK
UKHW052052250619
345024UK00011B/214/P